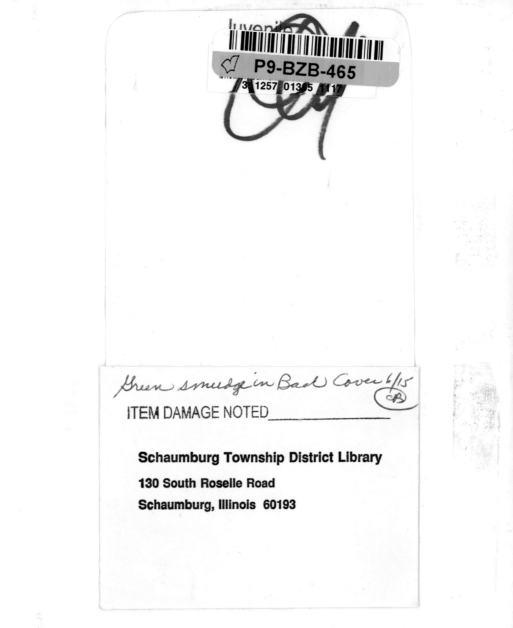

Ferns

By Allan Fowler

Consultants
Martha Walsh, Reading Specialist

Jan Jenner, Ph.D.

ΦΡ Children's Press®
A Division of Scholastic Inc.
New York   Toronto   London   Auckland   Sydney
Mexico City   New Delhi   Hong Kong
Danbury, Connecticut

Designer: Herman Adler Design
Photo Researcher: Caroline Anderson
The photo on the cover shows ferns growing in the wilderness.

Library of Congress Cataloging-in-Publication Data

Fowler, Allan.
    Ferns / by Allan Fowler.
        p. cm. — (Rookie read-about science)
    Includes index.
    Summary: This simple introduction to ferns discusses fronds, spores, and where ferns grow.
    ISBN 0-516-21687-2 (lib. bdg.)   0-516-25984-9 (pbk.)
    1. Ferns—Juvenile literature. [1. Ferns.] I. Title. II. Series.
QK522.5 .F68   2001
587'.3—dc21

                        00-055573

Plants do not grow feathers.
But a fern looks like it does!

Ferns have leaves that look like feathers. These leaves are called fronds.

5

Ferns are a lot like other
plants. They need good
soil and water to grow.

But ferns do not grow from seeds. Ferns grow from spores.

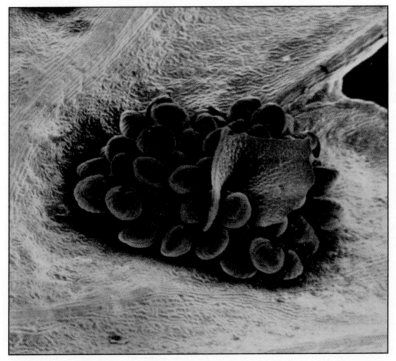

Spores seen through a microscope

Spores are found in cases
under the fronds of a fern.

These cases look like
brown spots. One brown
case holds many spores.

10

When the air is dry,
a case of spores pops
open. The wind blows
the spores through the air.

If a spore lands in a damp place, it can grow into a small plant.

This small plant is not a fern. It only lives a short time. But a fern will grow out of it.

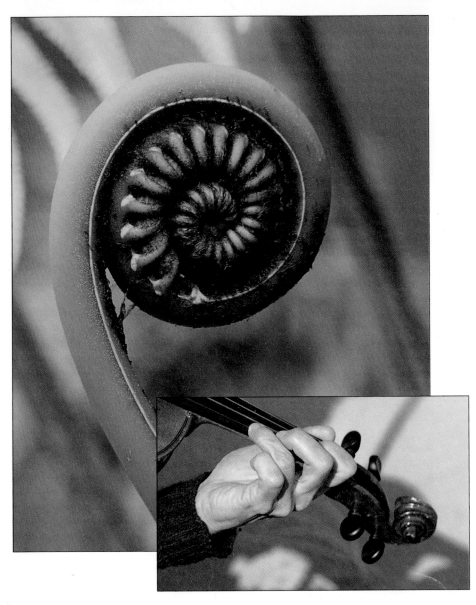

The fronds of a young fern curl up at the tips.

This curly tip looks like the end of a violin, or fiddle. That is why young ferns are often called fiddleheads.

As a fern grows, its fronds unroll.

Some ferns grow to be very tall.

Tree ferns can keep growing until they are more than fifty feet tall.

Tree ferns have woody trunks, like trees. But they do not have branches.

17

Ferns are found all over
the world. They grow
in forests and gardens.

Most ferns grow where
it is shady and damp.

Some ferns grow near
the sea. They grow in
the cracks of rocky cliffs.

Other ferns grow on trees.
They never touch the ground.

Bracken is a fern that grows in many places.

Animals, such as deer, like to eat bracken.

Bracken turns brown
in the fall and winter.
It becomes green again
in the spring.

Other kinds of ferns stay green all year long.

People grow ferns indoors.

You may see them in homes, restaurants, and schools.

Are there any ferns in your classroom?

Words You Know

bracken

cases

fiddlehead

fronds

spores

tree ferns

31

Index

About the Author

Allan Fowler is a freelance writer with a background in advertising. Born in New York, he now lives in Chicago and enjoys traveling.

Photo Credits

Photographs ©: Corbis-Bettmann: 20 (Michael Busselle), 27 (Macduff Everton), 24, 30 top left (Richard Hamilton Smith); Dembinsky Photo Assoc.: 25 (John Gerlach), 19 (Michael Hubrich), 20 inset (Rod Planck), 8, 30 top right; Dwight Kuhn: cover, 3, 9, 10, 13; Photo Researchers, NY: 7, 31 bottom left (Biophoto Associates), 29 (D. K. Purse), 5, 31 top (V. P. Weinland), 18 (Roger Conant Wilde); Superstock, Inc.: 6 (Charles Marden Fitch), 26; Visuals Unlimited: 14 inset, 17, 31 bottom right (D. Cavagnaro), 21 (Mark E. Gibson), 14, 30 bottom (Mark S. Skalny).